BEAUTY IN

ALL I SEE

Photography and text by
Connie Moisson

*Leanna
Enjoy the beauty
around you where ever
you go.
Connie
2006*

ISBN : 1 - 59152 - 028 - 2
Photography copyrighted by Connie Moisson

Produced by Sweetgrass Books, a division of Farcountry Press
P.O. Box 5630, Helena, MT 59604

Created, produced, and designed in the United States
Printed in China

Introduction

Hi, my name is Connie Moisson and this book is the result of my passion for nature and photography. In April, 2004, my husband, Rene, and I sold everything we owned in Illinois and bought a 30 ft. motor home and decided to work in National Parks. Yellowstone National Park was our first destination and proved to us that we had made the right decision. Waking up each morning with the beauty that abounds in Yellowstone was worth all of the material things we gave up. The strings that tied us down while owning a home prevented us from enjoying life like we wanted to. Now we can come and go and see nature at its best and not have to rush on to the next stop. I hope you enjoy looking at my photos as much as I have enjoyed taking them.

This book is dedicated to my late husband, Rene, without whose help, encouragement, support and love, this book would not have been possible. He died unexpectedly on November 26, 2004, which makes this book even more special to me. We made a good team when working on any project and his input and ideas come through in my photos. He made me believe in myself and my ability to take photographs that other people would also enjoy.

Connie enjoying the beauty of the Park in the winter.

Sand Hill cranes can be seen along the Yellowstone River. The mornings are cool and often a misty fog envelopes Hayden Valley.

Lodge pole pine trees depend on fire to open their cones, releasing the seeds from which a new generation of trees will grow. Looking around at the burned areas of the park, I could see new growth and wild flowers everywhere. Fire is a natural occurrence and is a major part in the life and death cycle of the forest.

In 1988, fire burned 793,880 acres of Yellowstone National Park. Today we see new trees growing throughout the area and the forest will be replaced as nature intended.

There are many bald eagles in the park. They are perched in the trees along the rivers that run through the park looking for their next meal.

Grizzly bears can be seen in the park if you are at the right place at the right time. Spring and fall are the best times to see the bears before they head to higher ground.

These pictures are more examples of grizzly bears that have emerged from hibernation and are looking for food.

The bull elk shed the velvet on their antlers in late summer. They rub their antlers on tree limbs to help remove the tissue. This process usually takes a day to accomplish so I was lucky to catch this one on film. I call this picture 'Medusa' because it looks like he has snakes in his antlers.

I had to photograph this badger in the top photo from a safe distance because they are very aggressive. The marmot in the bottom picture was more than willing to have his picture taken.

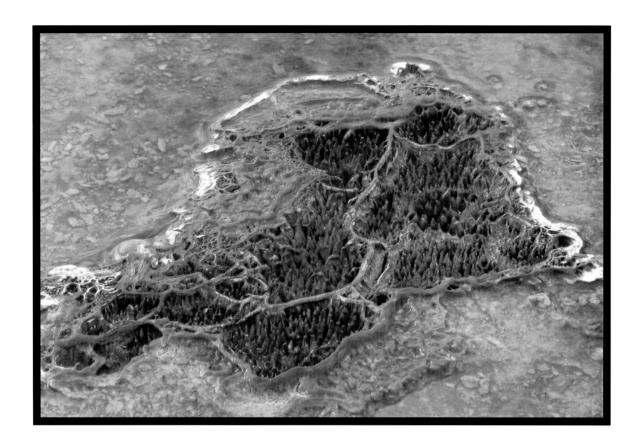

The algae in the ponds by the hot springs and in the run off areas vary in color according to the water temperature and mineral content.

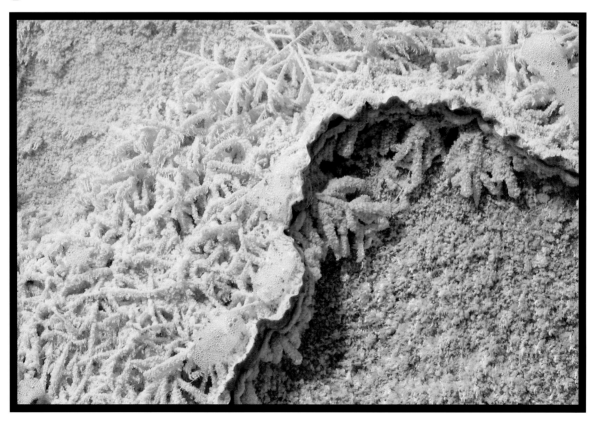

We liked to fish in Yellowstone Lake. One of our favorite spots was Gull Point. These pictures were taken on two consecutive nights. We would fish until sunset then enjoy the night's colors emerge across the sky.

The sun was setting and we had been fishing at our favorite spot when we saw this duck feeding off the bottom of the pond next to the lake. I was able to catch a drop of water running off her bill. Sunset is always a magical part of the day.

Mammoth Hot Springs is a place of beauty and color. The minerals in the ground come to the surface with the steaming water and are deposited on the surface to make large domes and formations.

Natural wonders are one of the things that make Yellowstone National Park unique. These are from Mammoth Hot Springs.

I enjoyed taking pictures of the coyotes. They weren't as elusive as the wolves and stayed around long enough for me to get their picture. We overheard several tourists say they saw a wolf, when in reality it was a coyote.

These geysers are part of the geyser basin at Old Faithful.   Clear hot water pools reflect the clouds in the sky and show a multitude of color.

In September and October you can hear the bull elk 'bugling' to challenge other bulls in their area. The bull elk will shed his antlers in early spring and the process of growing their antlers will start over again.

I call the picture to the right 'Elk Romance.' The bull elk is attentive to his cows and stays close by during the rut season. As docile and tame as these animals seem to be, they are still wild and unpredictable especially at this time of the year.

There is a large population of ravens in the Park. You will find them perched by a picnic area waiting for bits of food inadvertently dropped by people, or surrounding an animal carcass sneaking bits of meat when given the chance.

Nature's wonders appear before us at rare moments.

Big Horn Sheep can be found in Lamar Valley and on the hill sides between the north park entrance and Mammoth Hot Springs.

The pronghorn antelope are not seen as often as the deer and elk in Yellowstone, but small groups can be found near the north entrance of the park and in Lamar Valley. These pronghorn were grazing by the Roosevelt Arch near Gardiner, Montana.

The sun's early morning rays passing through the tall lodge pole pines paint a serene picture to those fortunate enough to see it.

The lower falls on the Yellowstone River are probably the most photographed falls in the park. At certain times in the morning you can catch a rainbow at the bottom of the falls. The upper falls in the picture below is also beautiful to photograph and to see.

Any time of the year, the falls present a beautiful scene. Most new visitors to the park are surprised by the sheer beauty of the falls. A lot of people believe that Old Faithful is the main attraction to see in the park, but I love the ever present beauty of the thundering falls.

Although these pictures look like winter landscapes, they were taken in the Spring. There is snow present in the late spring and early fall.

Birds are also abundant in the Park. On the water or perched in the trees they are there for us to find.

Wolves are here in the Park if you are lucky enough to get a glimpse of them.

Thermal features are found in many different areas of the park. Monument Geyser Basin is located high on a plateau, where after a hike in, you are rewarded with an unusual sight. Steam escaping from the chimney formation sounds like a breathing giant. Fountain Flats thermal area also offers spectacular features as shown in the picture below.

The Grand Prismatic Spring is a prime example of the colors created by the algae that lives in the run off water around the pool. Varying water temperatures create the wide spectrum of colors.

These pictures are close up views of the colorful run off areas of the Grand Prismatic Spring. Ribbons of color radiate from each of the pools.

Buffalo survive the harsh elements of winter, having to forage through the deep snow for the food they eat.

Snow adds an element of fairy-dust to the already breathtaking scenery.

Most people do not have the time to get off the roads and discover the beauty of the back country . Walking along Rescue Creek Trail near Gardiner, we found a wonderful fishing spot in the river plus the scenery was breathtaking. A lone elk antler lay along the trail as evidence of nature's cycles.

Early morning mist rises from the Yellowstone River. Conditions change every day, so the same scene can invoke different feelings at different times.

I have been fortunate to be able to see moose in the Canyon area and to watch the development of the calf through out the summer months.

This female moose has not shed her winter coat as the course hairy back shows.

I was very surprised and excited when we spotted this bull moose in a meadow near Canyon Village. He had followed a female and her calf into the area and seemed unaffected by our presence because we did not pose a threat to them by keeping our distance.

Imperial Geyser is a short walk, after you have hiked into Fairy Falls. It erupts every thirty seconds so you do not have to wait long to see it in action.

Deer are seen frequently throughout the park. The buck in the top photo and the doe and her fawns in the bottom one make quite a family unit.

Trumpeter swans are found on many of the rivers and lakes. They can be seen in the winter on parts of the Yellowstone River that don't freeze because of the warm water that drains from the thermal areas.

Elk lounge on the terraces of Mammoth Hot Springs as this bull elk roams the Lava Creek area.

Large animals such as elk and bison dominate people's ideas of wildlife in the park. I found these small critters equally fascinating to watch and photograph as they gathered their nuts and pinecones to store for the winter.

Autumn shines bright with colors of gold and green.
Snow is starting to accumulate on the mountain tops.

This buffalo calf looked like he was going to protect his mother from us. The bottom picture shows a Yellowstone traffic jam. The buffalo go where ever they want and the cars have to give them the right of way when they travel on the roads.

The presence of snow adds new challenges to the buffalo's existence. Deep snow in the winter makes finding food an extreme hardship. The buffalo's heavy winter coat and highly developed neck muscles, which they need to forge for grass, help them survive the long Yellowstone winters.

Being able to observe grizzly bears is all a matter of timing and being in the right area of the park. They frequent certain areas more than others so knowing where to look is helpful.

On a dirt road out of Gardiner, Montana we came across this small pond with an old building on it. Reflections of solitude comes to mind.

A black bear is pictured in the top photo and a female black bear and her cinnamon cub are in the bottom one.

Fishermen from all over the world come to Yellowstone Park for a chance to fly fish. What wonderful surroundings to have while trying to outsmart the cutthroat trout. I learned a lot about the science behind fly fishing and have decided I'll stay with the spin casting rod.

You never know what kind of wildlife might greet
you when you enter the North entrance of the park.

Winter conditions add a new dimension to the beauty of the park. Snow covers the area like a blanket and a wonderland emerges. Waterfalls have always been one of my passions , so being able to photograph this one at different times of the year was an added bonus.

The roles of predator and prey was shown as this ermine killed the rabbit and then buried it in a snow drift to keep it away from other animals who would take it such as the coyote and magpie below.

Last but not least is Old Faithful

Last but not least is Old Faithful